Psalms for Dogs and Sorcerers

Psalms for Dogs and Sorcerers by Jen Coleman
Published by Trembling Pillow Press
New Orleans, LA
ISBN-13: 978-0-9887257-4-4
Copyright © Jen Coleman

Typesetting and Design: Megan Burns
Author Photo: Allison Cobb
Cover Art: David Hart
Cover Design: Unsinkable Design

Trembling
Pillow
PRESS

Psalms for Dogs and Sorcerers
by Jen Coleman

Bob Kaufman (1925-1986)

detail of woodcut by Kristin Wetterhahn

WINNER OF THE 2013 BOB KAUFMAN
BOOK PRIZE
SELECTED BY DARA WIER

Psalms for Dogs and Sorcerers

by

Jen Coleman

For Devon
Who is a wonder!

[signature]

CONTENTS

APOSTROPHE & SOLILOQUY

NYC

PROPINQUITY

PSALMS FOR DOGS AND SORCERERS

APOSTROPHE & SOLILOQUY

Metal Helmets

"You had me scared for a moment God, I thought you were serious"
— Bob Kaufman, from "I wish…"

In all my human history angels
stake out my corporeal body
like a dog house, clutch purse,

moth winged angels, yellow moon faced
in their metal helmets.
Shimmer edged angels

weave a veil of flesh over my face.
Sometimes I hold my mouth open
to stop the voices.

We don't talk openly of metal helmets
or symptoms. Never ask angels
to explain the truth, they pay attention,

wander through the mind with a flaming sword
making decisions nature never made.
My life as if it exists seems

teeming with flutters
from deep, giving birth to perfectly
comfortable angels.

Gasps in Data

I go weeks without being reminded—
I was a princess witch
despising my tongue in my mouth.

There are many princesses in long skirts,
mirror princess, moon princess, baby princesses
touching in a friendly way

taking an elbow in the crowd,
cone hats with flowing ribbons,
princess, sister to a princess, sister to a princess

and they dance with their palms together—
heads swiveled like a ball joint,
cone hats spiral towards the queen.

I was a princess witch, and I wore a prosthetic forehead,
my forehead's skin grafted to a steel plate,
my steel forehead grounded with a green wire.

Princess ribbons tangle and release like a seaweed tide.
Princess beliefs unfurl, princess curls, I see—
dance matters, behave like a moon, believe like a moon.

Babies believe they see mirror-babies believing.
To this a princess is vulnerable, vulnerable too.
I was strange, I happened in a mirror.

They wear hats in tall cones,
the hats that make princesses princesses,
with flowing ribbons and sleeves.

I was the only princess
with a real cone-shaped sloping forehead
not giving in to morbidity.

Hey Lady

Hey lady, hey little white slipper. Nice coat,
nice coat. Hey naughty ink blot, nice bad wrestling,
I like your coat. Tell your daddy I touched it.

Hey naughty sex candy blood, how'd you get mind control?
Can any kid get it? Did you find out about my wife?
I'm trying to blackmail her out of her science.

She'd break my fingernails just to see if she could.
Haven't seen her in 22 years and the old neighborhood
mafia's just waiting for the next flicker

to tear my arms off, squirmy and wormy, squirmy
and wormy, all these bikers in white tee shirts
throwing the undertaker out with the worms.

I'm not conservative but I'm not much of a risk taker.
When the barber in Ballston Common comes at me
with a camera, about the weirdest thing I ever saw:

I could root right into him, root, root my dark angle
into his invisible pants. Leaky corked bottle,
cold yuppie plumbing, Neil Diamond's dirty fingernails.

"For god's sake," I thought to myself and now I'm thinking:
"Shit! This is a special gift! Twiddle the pants, hello ankle bone!"
Makes me sick all over America

and all you're left with's a pair of shoes.
I'll give you a hundred to watch.
You sure look nice. Friendly face in a crowd.

Angie in Sheboygan

I've got apple eyed visions of Angie in Sheboygan.
I've got sweet pepper visions of Angie.

She's pretty like a rock face, a thunder cloud.
Cream cheeks, she glows, she's a volcano
got hair like a wild mare.
Angie's flank is mean and strange as a wild mare.

I've got hankerings for Angie in Sheboygan
though they don't feed the horses like onions do
I've got apples in my pocket for Angie.
I've got a kercheif in my pocket for Angie.

Angie's nose is an arrowhead
sharper than her bare teeth.
Her smile's a wicked picket fence.
She was drove from a place she maybe knew
to this place, swimming with voices.
Angie's air is swimming with true voices.

She outwaits the poisons,
her mouth lipsticked with charcoal.
She bares her teeth at poison
lips peppered with ash.

I've got visions of Angie in Sheboygan
she's a banana gone bad.
Angie's got visions in Sheboygan
She's discovered her roaring blood.

My Friend Icky B

My friend Icky B is nourished by the glow
running like a river through tissue, muscle or bone.
Give this drunk a tin cup and he and Jim Beam
don't need your point of view.

But the whisky she's a risky destination,
and yet another beer truck lurks around Icky B.
He's losing everything around his arms.

Undocumented hazmat, baby, hauled vessels,
a shot-and-beer man ends up in a drastic emergency
drunk tank, built for a lack of other options.

Icky fronts a boiling teen-ager honky tonk band.
He brought his suit to the pawn shop,
baring his skin-honey spread-cloth of an ass.

Icky got drunk from touching a hot few crotches,
exposed, woke up in an Armistice Day blizzard.
Minnesota burn shock, Icky stands among the dead drunk
in the dead of winter, hops
on one foot in the outlying broccoli fields.

Icky's the color of the third degree,
a rambunctious smirk stapled in place.
The fluid in his blister is from Ireland.
He'll get drunk, fall down, and raise hell in your town.

Earthward Edward

Never better in the rest of the edge-
trimmed trailer, never better in the center
ring fight, fraught with peony-pink bruise blossoms.

So says the rest of the left-winged
test pilots, so says the nest of eagle chicks
flecked with frost from earth's chilling crust.

And the crust never stops on a dime,
never takes a toll, never rolls in a line of rilled sand
dollars registering red passion in the rest
of the wide blessed beach. And so goes the next

round, and the next round
with my young rebel's breast
checked for a costly crest,
checked for a costly cancer.

To dress in the linen of rest, the restless
at rest in the peony pink breast, the peony
chest burst in a nest, in a living nest,
never lost at sea, never lost

to the wicked rest of the deep and fathomless
foam in the fraught filled sea.

Book Shield

Bombings and battles and the war is over
with bombings and battles galore.
Waves of invasion and the war is over
behaving with waves of invasion.
Troops wrap the flag in camouflage,
camouflage wrapped in the flag.

And if the war were this way over it would
be at my door. The war at your door makes
you wear a shield: a book shield.

If it were a book shield before you
it would be in a field it would be
in a heather field where there
might be a grouse.

There is a certain sadness in the grouse
in the heather. There is hiding a certain
sadness to see the sky weather.

To see the weather turn yellow in the day
means a tornado. And if there were a
tornado at the door there it would be.

In this place, coming to this place,
there is a tornado and your skull will
weather it. You will weather it with your
head of hair. Your head of hair
here is a helmet.

I Am Delightful

I am delightful, and I know
what is delightful about you.

If there's anything
improper about a bald skull,
if there's anything
distasteful about a nude head
we shall not discuss it.

When I was a little girl, about 10,
they planted peonies for me
so dark they were almost black.

What you see in the shape of my eye
is not my eye,
sad and wonderful dainty boy.

This is the Next Time, But

often our blood feathers break
in a night fright, sparking

shark attention, and all the waves'
weight in the sweep of this sea.

Tooth and quill, born together
decaying toward elimination,

toward the water — no more
water.

NYC

Sunset Park

Today everything looks like a squirrel.
The marble angels in the cemetery, the pigeons
on the light post, the leaves hanging on the edges
of their tippling stems. Everything is all squirrel-nosed

and craggy knuckled for today, and the fur rough
and weatherproof on the edges of the car lot,
on the edges of the wrought iron gate and all around
the edges of tomorrow's leftovers in their to-go carton

of plastic and tinfoil. And when every dollar store
on the block offers a bushy-tailed gazebo planter,
there's no such planter in case of a drought
in case of a flood. Tomorrow is the day we'll talk

squiddily to the squirrels and what's squiddily
is squirrely in the ocean a squirrel in the ocean
a whirring squid in the ocean force gale.
The ocean force gale in the pocket of dire prediction.

Union Square

Words that generals fear
jail a journalist

plotting to topple rulers
with a charged word
warranted.

Watch who cares
for a word
when a journalist is jailed.

Watch while the word
goes free, flung loose
slipping onto the street.

Meatpacking District

In Manhattan today a moray eel wanders
the street sad and a moray eel wanders
the street sad and common and funny
and common she wanders, and she wanders

past a crock and she wanders past a hero
and she wanders past a window and somewhere
in that window there once was a cat
that bred and bred and then wasn't a cat

as much as a bag of cat bones
and if you are wondering where
the tea comes all into it
you can be sure the tea smells

like a ditch and if the ditch is running
along the side of the road there is water
in it and the crops run with water
and it is the great subway flood.

East River

So what does it matter, the ocean? What does it matter,
the ocean, when there's to be found on the land an island
where the buildings are canyons and it's a desert?
What does it matter to be a puzzled island

and we keep to the edge and the birds and bats love
the abandoned hospitals and the birds and bats have
a megacity home of clear water and babies, fat babies
floating on the East River barge pool, fat babies

of the East River barge full of a pool of fat babies;
what spectacle in the roiling water bed, water
colored of steel and in the East River a barge of babies lower,
into the river bed a rusty barge of gravel and the long claw

on a chain grabs gravel and lowers it to the bed
grabs gravel and lowers it to the bed of the estuary
the estuary a bed for a barge, a rocky
rocky bed for a barge pool of babies.

Brother Island

It's normal when groups of people die.
It is usual, in a year, for many to die
and become an impressive number. It's expected.

Day to day, when dead bodies are needed,
there are people like poppy seeds
in a muffin snuffed up under a collapsing circus tent,

the automatic fire of a tow-headed boy scout,
a burning cruise liner drops bodies bright and promising
like molten glass into the sea.

How many boy scouts have killed in a hundred years?
How many boy scouts killed? How many would-be
boy scouts but for the scouts how many boys

scout out scout boys for how many scouts
scouting killing boys scouts. How many
more boy scouts are living than have ever died?

Should it become ordinary, and some day
such great groups so often die
that there will be no difference

between limbs, jaw bone, mandible,
fragment of bone, the eye socket,
the chin bone muscle creating a face,

a jaw bone a living eye
and rows of even white teeth.
The expression of bone and body lost
in the company of other bodies.

Prospect Park

And the tornado hit Brooklyn and the tornado swept off
the roof, clean off the roof of the brick building
in Brooklyn and the car under the tree was a Lexus
under a Maple and that's a mighty old Maple tree

to take to lying down in the streets of Brooklyn
across the roof of a shiny Lexus. The tree
a hundred years old the Maple tree born
in a tornado a hundred years ago felled

in a tornado a hundred years later
and Brooklyn 1907 falls on Brooklyn 2007
and in 1907 in Brooklyn was there a tornado
there was a field there was a house there was

a twister and someone in Brooklyn was to see it
and someone in Brooklyn was very tiny to see it
in the Brooklyn that took up the wind that took up
in the wind of the Brooklyn tornado.

Bowery

Today there is a sore tendon,
a front of the shin pain,
a shin sin in the sin a shine
of splintering rage. Today there is

a mushroom in the crook of a tree,
a mushroom that grows on the outside
or a fungus that is an eat from the inside
kind of fungus — or it is a rye sandwich

and tomorrow a Thursday to remember,
a Thursday up there with the best
of the great breakfast Thursdays,
the ham and egg breakfast Thursdays,

the egg on a roll
and a packet of salt
Thursdays in the kitchen
of Manhattan.

Coney Island

The lust seagulls breed is not the eye,
not the scale-feathered bosom
or hollow-boned muscled
flap-flapping over crowds
for crusts thrown from meat-handed custard lickers.

The lust from fat gulls,
who are soft and close feathered, who are feathered
and mean, spreads across the shore
across beached thighs, a feast crowd
a catsup crowd, fried crowd.

Coney Island's tattooed Jesus
spreads sawdust in the freak show.
The passion show draws a fluster from crowds
with dark-adjusted eyes.
When our lord busts his skin
with a ten-penny nail,
he cusses.

The lust seagulls breed
wells over a low crowd, a beach crowd
of bright debris and ten thousand pale clam shells
shed in waves, in roiling miles
of balding, hairy oil-slick flanks
and a pair of crabs doing it in the water.

657 5th Ave, Brooklyn, 2004

Yeah you, year:

year of the wave,
the wave,
the hot
cold day close
shave brain wave.
You're not some
nuzzling year
mutely paying taxes.
You're a black
plastic bag,
lifted in the wind or crushed
in a gutter,
filled or heaped
or torn or held up

like something.

You're a milk crate
on the corner. How dented,
how non-stop discount,
how paper-cup,
how shave ice
diesel truck
how dead cat
swept crack of you.
And a stroller comes
sometimes to crash,
and a parking meter
wobbles.
And your empty bus
stops shatter, and

what is that?

Even your hot dogs
hot dog, your wieners
wiener. And if pigeons only
swerve, what more is there?
Your sewer caps be
as sewer caps of sewer caps
and seltzers be as
seltzer from seltzer
and there's rubber
soles on the street.

And there's rubber soles
on the fire escape
and in the shadow
of a bus stop and there's ants
on the drinking straw, and
the space between
cracks is the space
a crack is in.

And you, year,
your banana spoils near
a dark jump rope
and your spots rot.
Look, there's you:
you're a banana.

There:
by a jump rope
rotting, on the way
to Coney Island, whole,
split in the sun, crushed
under a tire, opened up
and rubber soles
rubber-side down keep on
keeping on going on by.

Flower Poems

for Carol

    after artist Michael De Feo's drip-flowers on New York sidewalks

1

Flowers bear a load
South of Delancey;
Pavement is passage for the public flower.
Those are load-bearing petals
West of Allen.

2

The latter flower
roots in foundry sand and fly ash.
Latter flower types:
Parking meters, road signs,
fire hydrants, bus stops.

3

Paint is half-painting is
half-painted is half-
flower is
half-flowered is half
observed is half-
seeing is half
eyelit.

4

What's a flower's function
in construction, for example,
or the gutter, or transportation,
or a glory-glow where the shadow would fall?
[Ca = calyx sepal whorl (Ca5)]

5

Grand street near Pike:
The paint is wet-shaped.
Some of the sidewalk moves
and the rest is intact.
Land plants are four-twenty-five
zero zero zero
zero zero zero years old.

6

There are a lot of lights-on-things
out there.
Mortar and concrete:
one meter for everyone
on Hester or Essex.
There's a flower to fruit up.
There are a lot of paints.

7

This rose
sets and hardens independently
enough to seriously crack
from the East River to the Bowery

8

Footpaths, footpaths, footpaths.
Twelve thousand miles of New York sidewalk
A low glow on Orchard and Rivington.

9

The sidewalk is
sticky.
The flowers float,
haloed, under the radar.

10
The earth \ moves beneath the sidewalk
all the time.
Five free sepals in liquid paint:
there is a wet-edge interval
called "open time."

11
Flowers are dependent upon
curb cuts, street lights, traffic poles,
the wind \ Others rely on animals
flipping the paint, dripping, or dipping
neighborhoods are strips of lighting.

12
A plaque to a prominent anarchist
is not usual. A gold ring of loose paint
cement-light. To bees,
a sidewalk. Not usual,
not for prominent anarchists.

What Matters

What makes a girl with a ring in her nose
think a girl worth the trouble
is different than a bee
blown among bees in a hurricane of bees
with a name, with a color like no other?

When people behave in a throng-behaving-
throng, they are dust motes
behaving like fear-struck dust.
They whisper without lungs
to a pulse propagating nerve-to-
nerve with unwavering shape.

No, a girl
worth the trouble is not a dust
mote trapped in the hinge
of the glasses of a passerby.
That is Fear: loud and invisible.

A Matter of Time:

There was the dream of the solder
soldier. Of reaching for the flux
and solder
and there is a soldier

and other dreams I call ridiculous
in the middle of the night--
I call it out: "ridiculous"

and out my window on the sidewalk
a howling boy with his hand
caught in the candy chute

his chubby hand
caught in the candy machine's
candy slot.

A Matter Believed to be Possible:

Don't reach up the candy
chute with your chubby hand, boy.
Don't throw your shoes
into the hanging canopy of shoes,

laces dangling over
the streetlight
in a community of shoes,
dangling, the streetlight adorned
with a whole leafy shoe throng.

Where are your combat boots? High above
fifth avenue. Dangling like a flurry
above twenty third street.

A Matter of Fact:

Other dreams I call ridiculous
are drawn to meet the ordinary,
normal, fruitful, capable
and purposeful demands
of angels in their self forgiving
wing cocoons.

They demand
successful wholes be made of
ten trillion cells, bacteria, gut flora,
skin flora, the inside of the eyelids
and other parts of the human biome
just like the four-faced angels:

at once a mountain lion
an eagle a flesh-face
and another not-visible face
potent in the people-waves
bobbing on the subway steps
and the tide's pull, pull, pull.
I turn my body over
in my sleep as if it exists
as if it is worth the trouble.

A Matter That is More or Less the Same as Other Matters:

Five thousand honeybees
swarm on the Epoch Times
yellow newspaper box

and the red candy machine
shimmering
a little bad in the sun

outside Fulton street station
under the blue construction
awning, docile and lazy,

halfway between the Hudson
clinging to Manhattan's edge
and the East River, aimless,

with its wharf rats
laughing ultrasonic chirps
full of hope

for the biology of their tradition.
It's a high bee count
in a mountain lion time.

A Matter That is Possible But Does Not Naturally Occur in Our Environment:

Gee, is that really a mountain lion,
I say, spotting the four-faced passenger
on the Downtown 4 train

with wheels within wheels
shrieking along a curve
under Spring street.

Is that a mountain lion? Gee!
I say it a few times.

And because language passes for truth
and order is disordered
the mountain lion
gives a long yowl.

A yowl with no audible answer.
A yowl: a model for words
at the very limit.
A yowl that demands physical integrity
even as some part of myself escapes
cohesion and falls to pieces.

Two Matters That Are Different in the Same Way:

If I'm not really listening
to hear things
not visible
in passers-by
where I travel,

it's what I am
if I'm the girl
with a ring in my nose
sorting out
my goods on the subway,

with a paper cone of sunflowers
or fries or sun-fried flies

in the eye of the soldier
whose camouflage boots
are marked AB Pos,
blood type on his heel.

The sun shines a little bad
and the breeze is still so different.

PROPINQUITY

If men are always guided by estimates of pleasures and pains, these estimates should be rendered as exact as possible.

A pleasure or pain, taken by itself, will vary in the four circumstances of intensity, duration, certainty and propinquity.

Each distinguishable pain or pleasure caused by an action must have its value calculated.

When this has been done for every person affected, and the sum of all the pains subtracted from the sum of all pleasures, if the pains exceed the pleasures in total amount, then the balance of pain will measure the evil tendency of the act.

Ward & Trent, et al. Volume XI. The Period of the French Revolution. III. Bentham and the Early Utilitarians. §7. The Hedonic Calculus. The Cambridge History of English and American Literature. New York: G.P. Putnam's Sons, 1907-21

I've been nursing a sole cavity all day.
Though the sun is warm in November and nobody
remembers to be scared we all need a little more

arch support when the sky falls twice in a harvest.
We all get weak despite the finest most stylish
shoe. Nowhere in Queens is a stranger

not well versed in religious uses of steel
toed boots. It's not heroic to watch the mayor
on TV, dust trapped in the hinges of your eyeglasses.

In Queens
a bird preserve
in the shadow of an airport
under roaring tails
of heat and smoke, shakes.
A thousand egrets
on mud banks
ruffle
among twisted shrubs.

In Manhattan
the mayor visits
the grand footprint
of the fallen hero
still smoldering.
The Battery Park people's
lapels
shine
with fiberglass.

In Jamaica Bay
a child casts his net
among dark, deaf herons.
The surface swirled
and jeweled with jet fuel
broke through and produced
a hundred
fish.
The royal touch.

I had a dream to pull off
my shoes. My biblical bare feet were white and fat babies.
Lover patted my soles and struck them: bare feet

are a sign of trouble. But how beautiful

the feet that fly above Jamaica Bay,
that cross the East River,

that walk dusty shoes in hand, that emerge

from rumbling concrete, that carry lovers
whole through the door.

If the foot were an organ of touch
If below the sway of legs on a train
If barefoot and gracious the world at our feet what would stink.

The untrammeled feet of natural man do not stink.
A room full of barefooted plan makers do not naturally stink.

Nations conspire and people plot in vain;
they contend not against flesh and blood.
If your foot causes you to tread on lion and adder and stork
the young lion and serpent and stork trampled underfoot
if your foot, world rulers of present darkness, if your foot
is not shod with peace and love undying:
cut it off.

Mary Magdalene true to her psyche cut the soles from her
shoes and Mary like Teresa was barefoot. Mary like Teresa was
discalceatus and Mary like Teresa was nudpieda and Teresa Mary
bare Teresa foot barely Mary and who was not pregnant barefoot.

For every piece of footwear ever in the elevator in vertical commute
For every foot shod against shame as a foundation,
pillar for the brain
For every foot made weightless in fear and collapse

The answer to setting limits on faith
The answer to missing the point the truth past the mask
The answer the distracting destructor is obvious: go barefoot.

Fix a fresh meal.
I bought a bluefish. Though I might prefer the sparkling eye

of the farmer boy's trout, the Queens boy's
unfathomable shadow, the sea depth, the abyss
drew me to his olive, fatty fish.

A great blue heron   one knobbed leg bent,
bones of the toes curled to a withering burr,
        a twig breaks,
the great tent wings spread the bird
out low over the water.

The big toe important for walking.
The one that doesn't curl.
The one presses against tumble into flight.

Each step each note in a song.
Beautiful feet promise soft steps
promise curling toes soft on the nerves
        wise step wise move a day inside
a day in the inside world olive bread sweet
warm bread of honey promise
plenty of oil
and bread action in the eyes a mending gift
a threat a muse a disaster ruin shame grief.

Throngs pass from the smoking city in wingtips
    feet inflexible levers
coerce the bridge to move bodies forward.
The wingtip does not stumble though the ground
now no longer can support what they know to be true;
a wily brain and crafty plan weighs even
only on the ground of what's come before.

Saint Teresa walked barefoot from Spain to Rome
though she didn't speak of it how else
might she cross distance look at her strong feet
like carpenter's hands throw a contemplative order
of barefoot nuns into the red dust.

The airport enters the sole of my foot
running down the inside bump of ankle
to the underside. This twinge bends my leg
like a heron. Turn my foot inward.

What good will off-ramps be when the human foot is the only safe
locomotion. The city carves out supple soles alive.

The dirt holds eight immutable truths:
1) the give in the ground is a small gift
4) a dirty sole is a blessed shame
7) anyone who sets off running will learn how to run in comfort
5) when the sky falls arches can't save you
6) children who play unshod learn balance
8) the lower extremity is inherently durable.

In Brooklyn a pigeon flock mirrors
the sun down from blue
like paper tumbling in a plume
and nobody sees the twitch outside
of my anonymous feet
how I walk and my shoes.

Twenty four feet of faithful sheep
in the midst of wolves shake off dust and leave the city
hoping angels will bear them up
lest they dash a foot against a stone.

Distracted soles in slack cheeked shock
put off shoes in dirt long poisoned
the foot a marriage a wiggling of life
among worms tapping to wet bones
Quakers long buried sift the quakes of dirt
to the sole and be moved.

Angel directing an angel told the mayor take off his shoe
and walk in the rubble while the FDNY shoes hanging from their
necks feet bleeding to the pier where Battery Park exiles wash
feet with tears and wipe with their hair exiles in acrid air
loosen the shoes and spit.

Demolition loaded from crane to barge
in sleepy or rushing waters
by idling or roaring trucks the barge
of steel and rock pierced with bone
towed off to Freshkills or Pennsylvania

over brown waters over snapper rockfish
over sole truly good for you and your heart
and your heart pierced by splintered trout
bones murky swelling abyss holds nice big bones
without sinking where small bones settle
on the water where small boned fish flicker

raw feet lewd as fingertips
without panic. Push the world fro.
How well bare feet grip grief.

I've seen salmon leap to water 20 feet or so 20 feet deep
the ground there runs ground water the sole
source aquifer no alternatives
features of generations in wealth of rock.

To the manufacturer of the solar system
that designed feet send
all the blinding heat to the sole.

To buy some new boots,
leather with ample calf.

To be barefoot marks obedience to terror
obeisance to dangerous sky treacherous fields.

Generations have trod have trod have trod
 in the burn of life that our foot cannot feel.

Pale and stylish never see feet
toe the sharp edge of hunger
and surrender ones body to market.

This little piggy on the ball of a sole;
this little piggy where unguents flow;
this little piggy ate the oily mud;
this little piggy curled in.
This little piggy cried memememe
until the ground collapsed 6 stories deep.

PSALMS FOR DOGS AND SORCERERS

Theory of an Afterlife

I'm a balloon dog, you
have a reputation for kindness.
I'm doomed, a balloon dog,
kind of a kind.

I have the world and worry about it
the stripes of a bigger tiger
I am a balloon dog and
I love the soil as myself.

I am a balloon dog,
My babies walk into the sea.
A balloon dog, I'm the only
one again again.

I am a balloon dog I insist.
I wish for peace
I send you a kiss.

I can see you clear as a rock.
Once, if you thought
you knew a balloon dog
it must have been me.

Fragile X

Cabbage is green. A pretty bowl is green
is fragile. She is
an embarrassed elephant. She is kind.

Green kind is a kind she likes. Her eye is
a fragile ball. Kind
is a pat of butter. She is an elephant

who can find a fat mouse. Fat Mouse plays
a fine game. Marbles
is a game she plays with marbles. Ten is an X.

Ten tells how many. Ten cabbages are
a fine ball of leaves.
Elephants find things that cannot really

happen. She can squeeze juice from most fruits
and vegetables.
The shape is called a heart. She can squeeze

but when you get hurt you see some of your
blood. She sees a fat
mouse a pretty green bowl in her eye.

Not many elephants see a human
bone. This is not
a pirate flag. Bones make a fragile X.

She is an embarrassed elephant.

Doesticks

This once-stolen baby in coat tails
this old baby wagging a wool tail
flings an elbow,
oh grass,
flings an arm
at the night.
Rouse a body
lick a body just born
a live thing fresh out.
Let them tango
by a sulfurous lake
let them tangle
by a stink hole
relieving a fiery foot wound
re-living a most furious wound
in the air mighty
in the air incensed
in the air
with cricket thunder.

Locusts and Wild Honey

Let the sea colored eels teem with urchins and worms,
and let the orangutan with mad mouthing tongue
fly above a slurry of swifts in the sunset
and into a clutch of centipede eggs curled coy
in the middens of the whitebark cones
come to feed the Douglas squirrels that feed the big
brown grizzly all the way down to Idaho.

And let a rat be a short-eared bunny
or just a rat in a short-eared universe
and the bicyclists after their chicken-catching kind
swell their hearts too and feed the river cats
near the railroad track and let there be future
farmers among the pigs and sheared shropshire sheep
and kind of a baby cow and miniature rams.

And let all be fair in the hay and sawdust
and in a serious storm of being aliveness teem,
according to a kind, and to every sea horse
a black tongue according to its kind and good,
wild medflies after their kinds, sassy potatoes
with corn dogs and buttermilk after their kinds
and all koalas that clutch according to their kinds.

And one kind hungers after another kind in accordance
with past nature, another kind takes after yet another
kind in kind. According to creatures, this is kind
of a kindness time after time.

Soothsayer

You are the ward of a word and the word is you
who would stoop for a crumb of light.
You are born of a word and the word is flesh
and small as a snowflake, small as a pill,
a brain pill, a smart pill, a thrill pill, small
as a get thinner faster pill, a youngness pill,
small as a cigarette pill, a lying tongue
pill, born of a word small as a parking meter

pill, a dead pigeon pill, a haughty pill,
a ram sacrifice pill, a spirit pill, small
as a pill to stir up dissension, small
as a normal pill a moral pill a patient pill,
a letter of recommendation pill, a pill
promulgating anew, a pill in the valley
of the shadow of death, a pill of majesty,
a pill of salvation, small as a steadfast love pill,

a pill to please the lord more than an ox
a pill incapable of pleasing god,
a glad heart pill, a cradle pill, a shame pill,
an innocent blood pill.

You are the ward of a soft tongue
that would break bone.

Via Not Non-Affirmativa

God is a god. God
is not a god. God is
not a non-god, a not-god,
not not a non-god god.
God is not non-one.

God is not non-real and not non-bigger
and not non-mother and not non-father
and god is not not-in-the-constitution
and god is not non-identical with the world.

God is not not-back not non-in-charge
is not not taking to the airwaves
not not within you
is not not as close as breath
god is not non-what-god-does.

God is not not non-partisan
god is not a non-war god is not-not peace-is-love is not non-red
god is not non-smiling not non-speaking
 with a not non-mouth a non-mouth too.

God is not non-impossible
and god is not not a word and god is not
not a non-word
and not not a verb and god is
not not an utterance not not the answer.
God.

Animalcule

If there were a rugged red squirrel in you
a rabbit, and whiskers;
If there were a crimson porcupine in you
It would be brush-foot, and gnawing.

If there were a second jaw in you
A toothsome pharynx double-bite;
If there were a mouth deep in your mouth
It would have talons, hook-like, sharp.

If there were a planet in you
A world of a sphere and orbit
If there were a planet of you
It would be meadow and ocean.

If there were a steel robot in you
It would be funny.
If there were a river
Swirls and eddies of thrumming fish.

If there were a city of birds in you
If there were a marble in you
If there were an estuary,
If tornado, if a crop,

> If there were a you
> deep in the you of you
> If you were truly in you deep
> It would be so, too.

Reward Reword

The ducking rabbit leads a party out, leads
the ducks out to spin on the spindle center
of the pond, a scent of duckweed
and a rabbit spinning.

In a duck pond that's a party of clever peeping
duck-chicks paddling so circular
around the little black pond.

And where in the pond is the bullhead so caught
up in the flutter of feet it does not see
a rabbit, a wet rabbit, spinning in the center
with a foot of luck?

A foot or so of luck surrounding him,
the glowing bullhead is a party of one, a bullhead party
in the pond of one.

One where there are plenty, plenty for all,
where there is a rabbit and ducklings
and a bullhead and somewhere there
there will be feats.

Untoward Upward

If there is a beaver
there is a dam there is
a slack-water there
is a coho.

      If there is a coho
there is a cool seep
shadow of a riffle
there is a coho reared
in a slough of a reared
fur-born beaver.

Preparing the cool seep,
the lux-furred kit
fed on cattails
feeds a dawn aspen
to the slough

      to still the water
for a fine slim
silvered salmon.

Prepared in the cool,
the fish shifts its snout
to the salt-water
and is sea-bound.

SUMMER

Heat song

The bees all know and long and curly
tongues and the lilies all know waxen
and wobbling honey in hot low.

Summer comes in; cloud of princes
builds a town; knowing weather
from the wet blue lasting lilies
in the low a nectar judging honey.

Young lilies hug up; young
lilies nap in wax skins; old lemon
and blues.

Low steady weather coming   the swell breaks petals
and rains bounce stamens lemon
and blue wet. The summer beats hot.

Thunderstorm song

Unshaven afternoon and angry cats.
A storm sky, a barn left to winds
a carnival of danger a slackjaw miracle.

Beaks shine like a skull
across the landscape.
Best ways scream into focus.

In absent exhaustion to sleep
as fish dip noses into the air.
Bony moss snouts tip the surface.

The passing year looks on
as the clock does its best to turtle
there, a wooden judge, a cop

a mewling monster
a realistic chance devouring
the air and anybody loitering.

Sparrow song

Wild wheat sombrero, whiskey neat—
a ring side gutter suite,

wild whiskey ring side gutter suite—
spare my church sombrero, chap.

Sugar beet, sugar beet, straight up whiskey neat.
Steam heat churn, tweed and blare, oh,

churn and tweed sombrero hitter
balloon seat chopper up main street

chew and churn, outwit pharoah
pharoah up main street cheap sombrero.

Whiskey neat, cheaters churn butter.
Butter cheater cat's feet

spare arrow hitter cheater
wild wheat chap, spare arrow chap.

Song on the End of the World

Bee in a junky old shop on a dusty old shelf undisturbed by the
threat of a heavy old leaded glass mirror that totters beside it a
bee, bout the size of a thumb it's a bumblebee bear of the bee
world. Growling its wingbeats it lifts from the shelf like a
passenger 'copter or tank, it's an ancient machine or an alien airship
with millions of tiny bee people inside, and it flies with its landing
gear dangling like roots, and it lights on an iron meat grinder
and settles, its abdomen lively, its shiny black shells overlapping
and heaving pneumatically under its fur like a field of black grass,
yellow wheat, pasture on bee-back, with dust like a pollen in sacks
on each stem of this bee oh this bee-bear a relic metropolis under a
shell it's a bee-bear that's finally come for us all it's a bee-bear will
show us the way to the light, it's a bee-bear declaring the end of
the world it's a bee-bear that opens the door to the future a bee-
bear brings tidings of joy to the earth the beginning the end-all
is bumblebee bumblebee too.

Mirror song

See you see a bee-swallow hive, see
you see a honeycomb wriggle,
what's changed is the humming space,
what's moved is the wing become light
though the light is a space
that quivers and a magnet
and the sun is a hot glass.

Bee sees bees dancing and bees
See hyssop fields in a tunnel and honeycomb
eyes see hyssop hyssop it's me that's a lens
in a straying sky eye a bee sees
a bee in a hyssop a sparrow sees
bee broth of light a broth bright.

The mirror the way the mirror
what's not done a wand true wielding
a mirror named wizard the mirror borrows
the hyssop bees honey queen
sees honey queen and drone sees wiggling
drone and inside eye a trust mirror
perfect unmerciful face, the light
turns back the bees go in.

Lake song

The lake has its breathing the lake has its features
the lake has sturgeon a ship and a sky. The lake has
its weather the lake has its honor the lake has its
nonsense and ducks and its width. The lake has its
tragedy the lake has its mud the lake has its ocean
and lava and luck. The lake has its plankton, exotics
and bridges the lake has its lovers and dwellers and geese.
The lake has its beckon the lake has its flapping the lake
has its length and its bottom and froth. The lake has its
sewage the lake has its light the lake has its gulls and its
smells and a swell. The lake has its roar the lake pushes
its shore the lake has a fog and its ship-splitting rocks.
The lake has its alias the lake has its consequence
the lake has its people lowered onto earth.

Fire song

for Arielle

A girl come home to fire-torn trees
where a mountain burned and fell
thinks herself a queen bird in a stubble-mountain town.
Girl pretends to be a thinking-rock, turned up in a gown.

A born egg, cracked, dying, makes a sad girl think she was
born in trees, sad because a tree fell.
A wood, a woodpecker, years ago that always was.

Ash cruel, flash-ash she pretends to be
Asherah the trunk, Asherah a tree.
Beds dry in the sun, a mother being, a child to be.

Bare rocks, charred by birth, because
birth turns out a flood born in burnt trees.
A flood-wiped bed, a woodpecker with fiery skin
it looks like from where she was.

Burned beetles fell all, beetles fell all that did fall in the burn.
In the gully under the sun, a girl born to think did return.
Rootless char, a born egg, a year's skeleton.

A downed pine dry in the sun.
Dying never told a living of the sap of things begun.
Turn to the living, the living water bully in the canyon.

River song

I am trying to learn to learn
what matters to believe:

like a moon
like an eye
like children's cuticles,
half-moons, do.

The moth is a month, a mouth.
The river wears a groove, it proves a cove.
The possum poses a psalm, so fetch, so clutch.
Where there is a wolf, a leaf is in liftoff.

What I believe I see, I see:
a moth flutters, one with joy,
toward the moon
in the brimming river
developing its own strategy.

Night song

Not for the resounding in the night
the reason for a star strung with no sound
in the sung trotting
the trotting sound
of the song in the resinous night.

The resounding stick of the tock
and ticking clock is tucked under the arm
of the round-sounding bold bastard
the bold and loud bastard
in the resinous night.

The gummy clock in the star struck night
struck like a gong, a far gone clock
in the center of not-the-center clock
stuck with a fat found roundness
knee deep in the not-night dark
of the gummed sound clock.

If it weren't a reasoned tautness
then a reason taught in sticks
bold sticks of clock tocks
are dark flocks of brittle geese.

Dark and brittle-footed geese feather
in the fragrant night
flock far from the center
not-at-the-center of the resinous night.

City song

With clerical clothes and schoolboy shoes,
a coward passed the bar twice and twice
declined, twice traced a lip-read for next-to-nothing.

Odds a million—odds and oddities—a million
to one, twice-traced in the saliva frost on a
disco window.

A window to the disco shows the coward,
greatly familiar with steep odds and the
creaking boy with the past life.

Past the last life, a night might lie in a night
mind (might lie with a lip if the disco
supposed to creak a cleric-creak).

The boy has a loud lip with a lie in the night.
A loud and slippery lie, like a carp parked in
the lake deep under the frost (under the
sleek odd frost of an early freeze).

Doctrine of the Rude Dream

with Confucius

*

What the Milkweed Pod said:

What the Brain has bestowed
is the Rude Body;
this Rude Body is Naked.

Naked may not be left for an instant.

On this account,
the Rude Body reaches wide and far
and yet is secret.

*

What the Milkweed Pod said:

There is nothing more bone-tired
sleepy than what is secret,
and nothing more than what is bone.

Therefore the Rude Body
is watchful over itself, when it is alone.

*

Milkweed Pod said:

The Rude Body may be said to be
Pleasurable Disgust.

When those feelings have been stirred,
the Revolution ensues.

Pleasurable Disgust is the great root
from which grow all the actings.

*

And this Revolution
is the universal Nude
which they all should pursue.

Let the Nudes of Pleasurable Disgust
and Revolution
exist in a box of crayons,

and an order will prevail
throughout Brain and Earth.

*

The Milkweed Pod said:

The Moss-Back Turtle embodies
the course of the Dream; the Rude Body
acts contrary to the course of the Dream.

The Moss-Back Turtle embodying
the course of the Dream
is a Moss-Back Turtle.

The Rude Body acting contrary
to the Dream is a Rude Body,
and has no caution.

*

The Milkweed Pod said:

I know
how it is that the Egg of the Dream
is:
The knowing
go beyond the Egg, and the contrary
do not come up to the Egg.

I know how it is that the Egg
of the Dream is not understood:

The rabbit goes beyond it,
the Rude Body does not come up to it.

The Rude Body may be perfect;
but the course of the Dream cannot be
but a Moss-Back Turtle
with an Egg.

*

Pigeon asked about energy.

Pigeon said, "Do you Dream the energy of the park,
the energy of the socks, the energy of flight?"

Rude Body swinging; and not to squash:
this is the energy of the park.

Water on asphalt; and meet death without regret:
this is the energy of the gray socks.

That's how the Pigeon cultivates
a friendly Revolution.

*

Great as Brain and Earth are,
bodies find things in them,
stuff to be dissatisfied.

Thus, were the Moss-Back Turtle
to speak of a way,
no rabbit would follow, and a Pigeon would split.

The way of the Moss-Back Turtle
may be found in
rabbits and Pigeons

wiggling brightly in Brain and Earth.

*

The Nude is not far from Body.

In riding a train,
the next subway is not far off.

Ride one train to set another following.

If we look askance,
they are the same train.

The Moss-Back Turtle
according to the Rude Bodies,

does what it likes done,
does it to others.

*

The Moss-Back Turtle does
what is proper to the waterfall she is.

In a squat of a flea market, she does
what is proper to a squat of flea.
In a poor and twisted chicken,
she does what is proper to a poor chicken.
In sweat socks, she sweats.
Among barbarous tribes, she barbers.

The Moss-Back Turtle can find
herself herself.

Thus it is that the Moss-Back Turtle is
while the Dream Body walks
in grey socks, looking for luck.

*

All the rabbits in the rabbit warren
array themselves in their richest fur.

Then,
like twisted water,
they seem to be over their heads.

Such is the dizzy.

Such is the impossibility
of repressing sincerity!

*

Thus they butt affectionately the dead

As they would have
butt affectionately them alive;

as ceremonies to Brain and Earth
they butt affectionately God,
who understands the ceremonies
to Brain and Earth, and the Dreaming

would find the rabbit warren
as easy as to look into the palm.

*

She who knows three things
knows Rude Bodies.

Knowing Rude Bodies,
she knows the rabbit warren
with all its families.

All who know the rabbit warren
with its families

know Pigeon-bodies of ink,
the mass rabbit children,
and indulgence
from a distance.

*

Self- with dizzy dizzy dress
not making a move,
this is the way for a Milkweed Pod.

Mooing moo, seducing rude,
making light midnight, and giving Pigeon to ink –

this is the way for Rude Bodies.

Giving them Pigeon and street,

this is the way for rabbit love.

*

Able to give fully her own Rude Body,
she can do the same to other rude bodies.

She can give, full of Rude Body
to animals and things.
Able to give full of Rude Body to creatures,
she can transform Brain and Earth.

Able to transform Brain and Earth,
she may, with Brain and Earth,

form a warren.

*

How great is the Nude!

Like over-twisted water,
it nourishes,
and rises up,

complete is its greatness!

The clear midnight of it,
and the earnest moo of it.

*

The Milkweed Pod said,

Let a Body be fond
of using her Body;

let a Body be fond
of assuming energy

of parks; let a Body
who is living

on the gray socks of all
act Rude.

*

The Milkweed Pod
is rooted in the waterfall
of the masses of rabbits.

Set up before Brain and Earth,
nothing in them contrary
to their waterfall.

*

The Moss-Backed Turtle is prepared to wait
for the rise of a Milkweed Pod
a hundred ages after.

Her being prepared to wait
shows that she knows bodies.

Such being the case, such a Milkweed Pod
twists the rabbit warren.
Her words for ages twist the rabbit warren.

Those who are far look longingly;
those who are near are never weary.

*

The Milkweed Pod
over her embroidered robe
puts a plain banana peel.

Just so, it is the way of the Moss-Back Turtle
to prefer the ink while it daily becomes brighter,
the way the Dream Body seeks notoriety.

The Moss-Back Turtle is to know
what is far is near.
She knows the wind blows.
She knows what is fond becomes ink.

*

The Milkweed Pod said:

Although the fish sink,
they are seen.

The Body examines its heart,
the Moss-Back Turtle
works with bodies that cannot see.

*

The Milkweed Pod said:

Look at your Body, be free from shame.

The Moss-Back Turtle,
when she is not moving,
has a feeling of truthfulness.

*

The Milkweed Pod said:

What needs no display is ink.

All the rabbits imitate it. Therefore,
the Moss-back regards brilliant ink,

making no great display
of transforming the rabbits.

*

The Milkweed Pod said:

Her ink is light as a hair.

Still, a hair is a pipe Dream.

Brains have neither sound nor smell.
That is perfect ink.

Yellow Tower Crane

After Yellow Crane Tower by Tang Dynasty poet Tsui Hao
(a poem of eternal farewell)

*In China, there is a Yellow Crane Tower on Snake Hill, once a
gathering place for poets. The tower was destroyed and rebuilt seven
times since the year 223 AD. Legend has it that, before the tower existed,
an immortal visitor drew a magic crane on the wall of a shop there. Ten
years later, the immortal visitor returned, and flew the crane to the sky.
Hundreds of poems tell the story.*

*In Portland, Oregon, there was a yellow crane tower at a construction
site near Director Park, a gathering place for poets. Erected in 2008,
the crane stood empty over the hole in the ground for 4 years while
construction remained stalled. In November 2011, in response to a
"trespass" lawsuit by nearby Nordstrom, the crane was deconstructed.
The site remains stalled: will the tower crane be rebuilt? One poem tells
the story.*

(translation 1)
Gone is the property magnate riding atop the falling loan market.
Here is the hardhat, climbing the Yellow Tower Crane.
The loans for glass and steel, once gone away, will not return.
The hard hat swings the massive crane jib away from Nordstrom
on and on, every month, a vain pilgrimage.
Pigeons atop rebar witness, orange-eyed and coo-ing
The for-lease sign weathers a thousand seasons
The sun setting, where is my Portland?
A 20 ton counterweight shifts in the wind
Nordstrom's landlord remains discontent!

(translation 2)
Wealth / departs / Yellow / Tower / Crane
haze / gaping / pit / Portland
Nordstrom's / sky / limitless ownership /
construction/ visit / pigeon/jib / swing/
trespass / averted / monthly /

(translation 3)
Big yellow tower crane jib left free
To swing over abandoned plans
Also swings above Nordstrom,
The sky owned up to heaven.
A low, loud, musical rattle –
A heavy and labored trespass.

(translation 4)
At the three-story deep construction pit
when the loan banks bid adieu
The towering yellow crane
compels Nordstrom to sue

Near Director's park, the crane's great jib
had swung too oft alee
And violated airspace
which y'all must know ain't free

a lone construction worker
resets the crane's vain course
there's nothing new, again, again,
the business journal reports

(translation 5)
Parking garage/ red max /Guild theater
For Lease /No Turns/ trees in pits
This yellow tower crane must go.
Unless, of course, there is a lease.
Nordstrom's airspace/ lending crane time.

(translation 6)
Here's our rich developer
next to the dream of a 33 story tower
for a hasty departure.
We're saying goodbye.
He's in a $50 million pit of unfinished construction
leaving a gaping, block-sized hole in Portland.
That lonely crane throws a shadow.
Now it is drifting over Nordstrom.
All you can see is that long, long jib:
Nordstrom's discontent with its trespass into light and air.

(translation 7)
Past promise gone
here remains a yellow tower crane
clear pigeon, clear eye
shiny granite fountain
day dusk Portland pass
misty construction pit
Nordstrom sues

SPACE AND OCEAN

The Time is Ripe

Humans must share
with marine mammals and sea birds
squid, krill, and one quintillian copepods,
the value of knowledge
for its inherent interest:
A Census of the Fishes.

A serious Census of the fishes
the prowfish the lungfish the glassfish
the blind sharks the blue eyes the smelt

onesided livebearers and the white eye
the jawless fishes, pinnipends,
count up the deep sea blob sculpins, snail and limpet

the blenny, the bonnetmouths and bonytongues
count the catsharks and false catsharks, brotulas and false brotulas,
count the lumpsuckers stuck fast to rocks

the dreamers and dottybacks, the gulpers and gunnels
the hingemouths and garfish with green bones
noodlefish, icefish, gibberfish and gar

naked suckermouth catfish count the ricefish
count rabbitfish, pigfish, roosterfish, and seahorses
count the puffers count milkfish count emperors or scavengers

fairy basslets, catfish, thornyheads and thornfishes
ribbonbearers, bonnethead, menhaden and ocean-basses,
jacksonshark, armored gurnards,

count up the lovely hatchetfish.
A serious census of the fishes
whether the wish exists.

Sea Water is Not Simple

Lowly are the foraminefera
among single celled critters, among slimes
and whip-like spinners, among diatoms, amoebas, green
single celled critters glowing in the hollow
hairs of polar bears.

Lowly are the forams, building their
shells from sea water in the deepest depths
to the brackish shallows,
stretching not-arms out
all across the sea, pulling

shells from water, stringing together
bits of brine into shells so superb, all
creature-kind with shell building
essences know many possible truths,
know all shells are good, and some

better, like heaven. And what is a life
of the mind if the mind is a cell
with a kind of life itself,
sexless like an angel with a plan
to build its own body from sea water,

a magnificent dead giveaway,
an open book, the tattler telling a
story of underwater weather with an intricate lack.
Is the single celled foram in the
water column what is and will be,

even as it rains down in death on
other foram with compassion
for hungry fish? The single celled critters
alive one in another, each building
a halo in the sea-mind.

Another Big Show Soon to Come

Lingcod play the role of 15 million unemployed
in this story. Squirrel monkeys play the role of the
carbon economy in this story. Squid will play the role
of the 46 million uninsured in this story.

Hungry lingcod sway in swells among pinnacles
in an earthquake by no other name than earthquake
off the fourth highest coast of unemployment.

Lingcod do not like dead bait.
Lingcod are the most curious fish by far
near the bottom of the battered economy.

The world takes notice of the lingcod feeling
jobless, the analysis, fish lurking
in the deep, making decisions.

Squirrel monkeys take notice of lingcod
with their "I'm still hungry" grins. Monkeys
see colors they weren't born with.

Squirrel monkeys see, in a triumph of science,
the heart of hearts burning, the chimney filling
the belly of the mountain.
In megawatt valley, with a hard won share of credit
squirrel monkeys know about nervousness
from the squid and its giant axon.

That a monkey knows. It knows from squid
from a red devil squid stalking fish up the coast.

Say it's warm, and squid swim
in the warm up the coast near the end of life.

Say the squid in the North are cold
and the end of their lives wash up.

Will a lingcod worry about a crippled
squirrel monkey worrying about
squid? The squirrel monkey
asks why its brain is telling it this and is telling it this
right now, this nerve, this educated nerve-ending
educated by a squid.

And the lingcod are all: "thank you squid
for showing science the mechanisms of compassion"
as hourly earnings rise a penny.

Weekly wages fall with outbursts and decorum.
Outbursts hoot-hooting in congress hoot-hooting
on the shore and hoot-hooting on the tennis court.

And the brain watches through the squid and that is how
the lingcod know the squirrel monkey watches,
and feeds itself a plum,
and feeds itself and watches and exclaims, and slides and claps
and watches the lingcod dart in a near-shore lair
dozens in 30 feet of water.

The squirrel monkey watches and knows
and if the monkey goes missing ask the axon
and it will or it will not tell.

And squirrel monkeys in another big show have coal at the heart
to burn, to see in red and green, a triumph
of science, in full color, as the lingcod refuse to let go.

A 50-pound lingcod bit and held on
to a 30-pound lingcod that bit and held a squirrel
monkey in its mouth,
even with the self-inflicted tailpipe affliction,
the *tacos del mar* affliction, the self inflicted
illness the lingcod holds.

Will the squirrel monkey seeing red bury the carbon
in the belly of the mountain and into the pores,
looking green and red
for curious lingcod to bite in the streets
and wash up on the cold beach on northern shores
where they've never seen squid before?

If it is not about race it is about rage it is not a race.
It is rage it is not a race to rage it is a rage
race. I do not mention
the president at all in this piece.

I saw only the squid chasing the warm waters north
to die on the shore and become picturesque.

Ode to Pluto

Mercury, Venus, and Earth and old Mars,
and Jupiter, Saturn, and one or two more,
there's four gaseous giants and four smaller round rocks;
there's asteroids, satellites, comets and dwarfs.

If the number were 12, but the number is eight
what exactly is truth when the number is changed.
The people are sad for the guy that's demoted;
the people are sad for celestial change.

Pluto's named Pluto the name is enduring
if Pluto named Pluto is a planet no more;
Pluto will spin in the stranger direction,
cross orbits with Neptune but never collide.

There's no planet X and there's no planet Pluto;
a lot of space objects are just the same size.
For seventy five years it's been Pluto named Pluto
its name hasn't changed it's a planet no more.

Astronomers are human and heliocentric;
astronomers are much more like Pluto than not.
A dad outlived Pluto's full run as a planet;
on Pluto a dad would be seven years old.

People are mourning the lost number nine;
it's the number that asks what we mean by the world.
Pluto is berried in time when it carries
a loose loop of orbit in good company.

Pluto and Charon, its fortunate moon
have mutual motions so far and away.
Pluto's a rock and its atmosphere's frozen,
and Pluto's a dog about the size of earth's moon.

Pluto bestows the dark hidden blessings,
and Pluto's angel-self saves the kitten and the day.

Reality changed, although Pluto don't know it,
the contrastiest body to orbit the sun.
Now Pluto's no planet its orbit loves Neptune,
its orbit's no circle its status is stripped.
Eight "classical" planets and Pluto's undoing,
eight celestial bodies reflecting the light.

Major planets accumulate all of their neighbors;
the planets eject all the mass of their friends.
Pluto it is nearly round, but not lonely;
it keeps its companions around and around.

Pluto has nothing in common with giants;
Pluto is smaller than some solar moons.
Pluto rules over the shades of the dead,
and Pluto saves the day by flapping his ears.

Pluto's still up there or down in its loop
as before it was named all alone in an aerie,
an egg among berries a bold egg in gauze.

Oh ever not alone it's a lush star-topped globe
 in a gauze of a posse of bodies in stars.
Pluto is rock and its atmosphere frozen
so far from the sun in perpetual dark.

Humans do care if it's Pluto in orbit
and NASA will be there in twenty fifteen.
Pluto's a god of both death and fertility;
Pluto's a dog on the trail of a mouse.

We won't say a planet or bone or an ovary;
we'll lay out the red rug for a not-lonely lump.

Onward Outward

for Sasha, even before we met

The difference between our world
and the world in the sixth system
is it is:

- as big as the sun
- with plenty of continents
- closer to its hot Jupiter
- orbit flat as an LP record
- orbit grooved and grooving
- with Neptune gravity-hands
- hands held out to parent stars
- with dinosaurs
- orbit a little more warm
- with cosmic perspective
- with continents afloat
- on a convecting fluid core
- with a dynamo

It's the sixth planet
in the system of planets
other than the one
with the world in it.

And the world's deep oceans
hold different continents and also the same
and orbits in systems
you don't know
and you don't know

anything about the world.

Straightforward Seaward

A bandit for the shore
poured into a suit of cockles

for shellfish supper, sword-fighting
at the subliminal edge

of the bandit-running nebula.
The swirling nebula at the shore

dusts the broad limit of the bandit's
whispering suit. The suit shells are cackling

in the nebula fog, in the fraught fog
of the edge of the earth. Where the earth

becomes a basin there is the right bandit
hideout. The fog-fire under cranes

at dockside, the shifting cranes, cast a bandit
shadow over the water and the bandit

rides a broom-horse across it.

Landward Leeward

If you steer the raft toward the edge
if you steer it into the wave with an oar
and pull a raft with a sail into the wave
(into the wind into the night)
it is a raft in the night.

In the three times dunking
(a dunking in occurrences of three)
in the occurrences, there is a corner.
In the corner there is an astronomical object.

A raft of hot Jupiters and a blonde sail
(the sail is blonde in the sun-like star of the night)
the blue sun-like star of the night is a shell
is a raft in the corner
(a raft in the corner of the ocean)
 pulling it like a quilt.

A roaster planet raft is pulling the ocean over it
like pulling a quilt off the corner of the bed
(a raft in the corner of the bed).
When the yellow is the night-time sun-like star
it is a thwarted dream.

The Hostile Policy of the Octopus

Sometimes it's easiest to let tentacles
do the thinking.

Sometimes in fatigue and pain,
or in the pain of solace,
or in the fatigue of hunger,
it is easier to let the tentacles
do the thinking and think it through
one feel at a time.

The red octopus is acting complex,
on the prowl, playing the game
without the consent of its players,
predicting the winner.

The red octopus pumps its
uncommon blood in the night,
unseen, wary, through three hearts:

a heart to profess opportunity,
a heart to discourage opportunity,
a heart to seize opportunity.
The ruby octopus sows uncertainty and doubt.

The octopus is a red and happy hunter
quenching its desire
with a pretty ugly mind,
analyzing the mood with its tentacles,
making little crabs lose their minds

Little crabs wave their eyes in the tide,
feel for shape,
flee from shape,
wave their clusters of eyes
and filter
a thousand
thousand cues.

Set from its first soupy cell to hunt
and decay, the ruby octopus trains
its tentacles
towards the smallest hermit crab,
predictably soft
with private legs
curled in a snail shell
going public only with its claws.

A cloud on the sand, the red octopus
cloaks the hermit crab in flashing red flesh,
drills a hole, delivers its venom
and prizes the tender body out.

The mission is to eat.
The mission is to maintain peace
from within a garden of empty shells,
—a freedom garden.

From within its den,
the red octopus increases
its arms exercise
in frequency and scale.

Sometimes it is easier
to let the tentacle do the thinking
and think it through one feel at a time,
like the corner of your lip grasping,
as if grasping were
the essence and the object of the prey
and you were the predator
grasping at the essence at the edge of a lip.

Common Anemone

> *Real solidarity means coming together for the common good.*
> *This Tea Party is real solidarity.*
>
> — Sara Palin in Madison, WI April 16, 2011

Beyond the fathoms of water, beyond
the kelp canopy fronds awash in salt,
beyond the weedy sea dragons' fluttering fins,

beyond the finger-like kelp roots
encrusted with purple urchins and sponges,
along the rocky reefs where black abalone cluster in crevices,

away from the dungeons of sea worms in tangled mats,
ashore from the plankton filtering sunlight,
out from the surge-swept pinnacle encrusted in orange cup coral,

bright in the clean sea,
from the memories of the sea long gone,
from the sea's memories, submerged,

from the warming waters
where the ten thousand absences awaken,
where the absences are stronger and more devastating than any,

as wrasses pick, startle, and pass through the gaze
of the giant kelpfish, schooling up—and then disperse,
I have a vision—yet by my ignorance, a hallucination:

The anemone are in a tidepool swirling with controversy.
Anemone, a century old, with their aggregates of clones,
discuss collective bargaining.

A pale anemone calls it the front lines in the battle for the future;
another points its tentacles to the line
drawn by the sea.

One anemone says
other anemone
wants to protect common power,

and another anemone says that's not real solidarity.
Real solidarity means coming together
against a common anemone.

Courage, says one anemone, is an anemone
standing strong in the face
of another anemone's thug tactics.

And that's what the anemone calls integrity.
And that's something one anemone
finds sorely missing in other anemone.

And another anemone becomes the scapegoat,
criticized as overfed and underworked,
unlike other anemone.

And it just seems that no matter what happens,
the barnacles become hungrier
and continue to kick their curly feet more and more,

and anemone all over the littoral zone are aggregating.
And barnacles can't think of anything more unholy
than the anemone that divide one into another.

 And then if an anemone is about to go dry and says,
"Hey?" The other anemone say,
"Oh no,"

"we can't change and are cemented to this
sort of teeny group of super anemone
that feels that no rules apply,"

"all the tide pool space should go to us,
and then the rest of the sessile creatures
should be stuck in the desert of sand beyond."

And that's why the anemone sting
other anemone into organizing,
scare anemone into trying to figure out

how to put their aggregates together,
to scare them into dividing in half,
forming smaller anemones into a large mat

of flower-throats, pink or lavender flower-throats
with their golden brown whips whirling in their tissue,
whip-whirling golden brown in the sun in the pool,

tubercles clinging to the rocks and sand
and shells they so choose,
so as not to lay bare in the ravages of an ebbing tide,

so as not to be lost
...
lost at shore

as a squid boat ghost ship is lost
swallowed whole by the sea
arriving as if to disappear

as the bones of the sea dinosaurs
vanish in the mountains of the abyss
where nothing is expected to be

to the wicked rest of the deep
and fathomless foam
in the fraught filled sea
where Medusa's face turns to dark
undefined by light, undefiled by light,
in the lightless night.

Collapse

Here's the way it is going to be.
The tiniest of collapses,
the collapse mostly dissolved
the collapse smaller than an eyeball,
smaller than a light, a speck of light on a speck of life,
this is the collapse dispersed,
the dispersed that is the collapse
the collapse that comes from the dispersal
of particles so small they are a code
so small they are encoded in the cells
of the homunculi that are making
what we are becoming, the most insidious collapse,
the cellular collapse,
the collapse at the
tiniest stub of being
smaller than an eye, smaller than a cell,
smaller than a hair on the cell,
this complicated combination lock,
this is where the collapse begins.

And it begins with a misunderstanding.
It begins with an epic misunderstanding.
An epic that is the story of the collapse
of a single being that begins
microscopic and ends with the end of life
as we know it and the beginning of something else
that is getting back up.

Whip an egg. Whip and whirl an egg,
and see what you get. That is collapse
that becomes a delicious dish.
That is a collapse that becomes a becoming.
But don't whirl the egg or change the egg
in a way that the egg knows it's changing,
and the egg grows, and the egg becomes,
and the collapse happens in the fat cells
turning to bone, or the bone cells

turning to brain, or the brain cells
becoming fat cells and all the while
the baby becoming a collapse of a sort,
a collapse of meaning, a collapse of
coherency, the kind of collapse that begins
when angels take over and start
throwing their weight around.

When the most dire of angels starts throwing
its weight around, when the most insidious
angels start throwing their weight around,
that's when we have invisible collapse
that becomes the zombie apocalypse.

And if the zombie apocalypse happens
below the surface of the ocean, and the water
of the ocean's surface continues
to reflect the sun nonetheless, it is the collapse
that happens as a zombie apocalypse
where maybe indeed there already were zombies,
where maybe indeed the zombies already did run wild
and swim wild in the wild upwellings of delicious life.

And now there is a change, and the change
at the tiniest level is leading to the collapse
of the zombies. An apocalypse for the zombies
as the zombies find a modest death and rebirth
and indeed in what way is this collapse
but for the collapse of the creatures
on the land and what they think that there might be
under the sea but will never know will now never know
because of the tiniest dispersal and the massive collapse?

Once there was a fish a little fish
and that little fish never really was one
not a one little fish but one among thousands
like a single body, and to see oneself
is only to see the other to the left and right and
south and southwest and a little askew

of right next to you, the little fish, the tiny fish
among fish that becomes a single fish
to and fro in the sea seeking the upwelling,
a sort of school of fish to avoid the big fish,
the big fish like a dark cloud with its mouth open,
the massive fish like a planet coming to swallow,
and so the self of the little fish in a school
disperses, and so the big big fish is only just
a little bit less hungry as the school streams
around and not in but only just a little bit
into the mouth the salty cool of the sea
the space between them the cool life of the sea.

And then say the big cloud is not a fish
but a dispersant, say, of the big globs of oil
becoming the tiniest and even tinier little bits
carbon little bits of hydrocarbon so small,
smaller than the little fish,
smaller than the space between little fish,
smaller than the space between the gills
of the little fish, smaller than the cells
that make up the gills of the little fish,
smaller than the cells in the gills,
smaller than the mitochondria which is
the little bean in the little cell
of the little fish. And then
even if the cool salt continues to flow
around them, then there is collapse.
Then the little fish do collapse.

Then they do collapse there in the column of water,
the water column so deep and unseen by the creatures
up there on land that so depend on the little fish
being little zombie apocalypse fish but no bit of feed
for a bigger fish on which to feed, on which the world
feeds, on which the people with the space between
them see one another but not as a whole
but as people parts and that is the problem
with the collapse.

Even as they are in the collapse the collapse
is in them. They are the collapse as the collapse
is in them. We are the collapse as the collapse
is in us. You are the collapse and you started
the collapse and who started the collapse
but a monster, it must have been a monster,
it must have been a monster we can blame
that has a whole lot of money. Kill the monster,
he made the collapse and he has a lot of money
and kill it and punish him punish the colla-lapse
that must after all be the hand of a monster
no matter how tiny. Disperse the monster.
Will you disperse, disperse the monster
in a little bit of a way, but don't let it
become part of my bone cells turning to fat,
my strong bone cells turning slowly but surely
to fat, the bone turning to fat, to fat,
to fat for food for fat. Fa-lapse, fa-lapse flap-apse collapse collapse
collapse.

Acknowledgements and Thanks:

This book is dedicated to my parents, poets Tom and Nancy Coleman.

Thanks to the Superfriends. Especially Allison, my partner all ways.

Thanks to Kaia Sand, Jules Boykoff and CA Conrad for encouraging me to put a book together.

Thanks to the talents behind all these fine publications:

Common Anemone and *Hostile Policy of the Octopus* were generated as pieces within the 13 Hats collaborative collective project in 2012 and 2013.
Census of the Fishes and *Psalms for Dogs and Sorcerers* appeared in Jacket 2, 2011
Selections from *Propinquity*, *Lake Song* and *Bowery* appeared in Elective Affinities, 2011
Another Big Show Soon to Come appeared in Capitalism, Nature, Socialism Volume 21, Number 2, 2010
Two poems appeared in Aufgabe #7 litmus press 2008,
Gasps in Data and *Mirror Song* appeared in EOAGH ISSUE #3, Queering language 2007
Ode to Pluto appeared in Observable Readings, observable books, 2006
My Friend Icky B and *Brother Island* appeared in The East Village v12, 2001
Fragile X and *Doesticks* appeared in Ixnay #4 in 2000

Jen Coleman was born in Minnesota in 1970. She earned a BA in Theater from Beloit College, and worked briefly at a circuit board factory, a three ring binder factory, a blanket factory, a gas station, as a theater electrician and as a schoolbus driver. She earned an MFA in poetry from George Mason University. There, she studied with Susan Tichy, Peter Klappert and Carolyn Forché. Her work was further shaped by the Washington, DC, poetry community. While in DC, Jen co-hosted with Allison Cobb a season of the DCAC "In Your Ear" reading series and completed a collaborative chapbook with CE Putnam and Allison Cobb entitled Communal Bebop Canto. Jen and Allison moved to New York in 2000, where they joined Ethan Fugate and Susan Landers in editing six issues of Pom2, "a journal of poetic polylogue." While in DC and New York, Jen worked for Environmental Defense Fund. Jen and Allison moved to Portland, Oregon in 2008, where they live with their dog, Quincy. In Portland, Jen participated in the 13 Hats collaborative of artists and writers. She co-hosts readings with the Spare Room Collective and works for Oregon Environmental Council. This is her first full-length volume.

Titles from Trembling Pillow Press

I of the Storm by Bill Lavender

Olympia Street by Michael Ford

Ethereal Avalanche by Gina Ferrara

Transfixion by Bill Lavender

The Ethics of Sleep by Bernadette Mayer

Downtown by Lee Meitzen Grue

SONG OF PRAISE   Homage To John Coltrane by John Sinclair

Untitled Writings From A Member of the Blank Generation by Philip Good

DESERT JOURNAL by ruth weiss

Aesthesia Balderdash by Kim Vodicka

Of Love & Capital by Christopher Rizzo (Winner of the 2012 Bob Kaufman Book Prize, selected by Bernadette Mayer)

SUPER NATURAL by Tracey McTague

I LOVE THIS AMERICAN WAY OF LIFE by Brett Evans

Q by Bill Lavender

loaded arc by Laura Goldstein

Psalms for Dogs and Sorcerers by Jen Coleman (winner of the Bob Kaufman Book Prize selected by Dara Wier)

Forthcoming Titles

Trick Rider by Jen Tynes

Want for Lion by Paige Taggart

Website: http://www.tremblingpillowpress.com

Made in the USA
Charleston, SC
08 September 2014